AND THEN THE SUN CAME OUT

Leading after Covid

Amanda Braden

©Copyright 2021- All rights reserved.

The content contained within this book may not be reproduced, duplicated or transmitted without direct written permission from the author.

Under no circumstances will any blame or legal responsibility be held against the published, or author, for any damages, reparation, or monetary loss due to the information contained within this book. Either directly or indirectly.

Legal notice

This book is copyright protected. This book is only for personal use. You cannot amend, distribute, sell, use or paraphrase any part, or the content within this book without the consent of the author.

Disclaimer Notice:

Please note the information contained within this document is for educational and entertainment purposes only. All effort has been executed to present accurate, up to date, and reliable, complete, information. No warranties of any kind are declared or implied. Readers acknowledge that the author is not engaging in the rendering of legal, financial, medical, or professional advice. The content within this book has been derived from various sources. Please consult a licensed professional before attempting any techniques outlined in this book.

By reading this document, the reader agrees that under no circumstances is the author responsible for any losses, direct or indirect, which are incurred as result of the use of information contained within this document, including, but not limited to, errors, omissions, or inaccuracies.

Contents

Introduction – The world is different now.

Leading after Covid- How do we lead differently in a world that continues to change and evolve in so many ways?

10 leadership challenges and solutions, through and after Covid

Part 1
Re-building the people.

1. Managing **anxiety**
2. Building **Trust**
3. Developing **Well-being**

Part 2
Re-building the team.

4. Adapting your **vision** in the new world
5. Treating people as **individuals**
6. Sorting the **conflict**, properly

Part 3
Re-building the business.

7. **Re-framing** what Covid has done.

8. New opportunities in a changing world

Part 4
<u>Re-building You.</u>

9. Taking a look at you- how **you** are doing?
10. **Developing** yourself in a changing world

Conclusion.
About the Author
Big Thanks
Sources

I.   Introduction

The world is different now.

The world looks different now, and it keeps changing, at times it's still surreal. We have been learning how to live with Covid.

One day we feel that maybe everything is better and fixed, and the next it's ten steps backwards to gloom and uncertainty. What has it done to our lives?

It was never easy to be a good leader on a normal day, and it's now harder in this new world. Our family, friends, colleagues, and teams are all learning, and struggling to cope in this same new world.

Are you a good leader?

How would you rate yourself as a leader in tough times?

- ✓ Are your people coping well, do you see a lot of anxiety in your team?
- ✓ Do you know how to help them?
- ✓ Do they trust you enough to talk to you if they are really struggling?

- ✓ Is your team working together well, or are they arguing more than usual?
- ✓ Do you see bad behaviour that you don't act on?
- ✓ Are you looking after yourself?

People aren't born as leaders.

They may possess the basic building blocks, interests, and ambitions, but their skills have the potential to develop and improve every day. Even the very best and strongest leaders struggle some days.

We can all grow into good leaders with the right support and help.

At tough times, as leaders, we all need to get ahead and above the challenges of our environment if we have any chance of success.

We need to learn how to lead, and help and support, in new and different ways.

Our abilities to be good leaders change and flux from day to day. Some days we're great and others we can be dismal. There is absolutely hope for everyone.

Life before Covid….

There were things that we could have done better as leaders.

We can all think of something that didn't go well. Or maybe we **avoided** the problem.

Covid has created **greater challenges** in some areas that we now need to work on. Those challenges are both physical and psychological. The global economic challenges are at a level not experienced for many years.

What's ahead?

We need to work out how to lead and work in better ways and, in some ways, differently.

In a Harvard Business Review article "A Time to Lead with Purpose and Humanity" Hubert Joly, the Chair of US company, Best Buy said

> "While the situation is somewhat reminiscent of the challenges faced during the Great Recession… There is no obvious blueprint to follow.
>
> But perhaps, the same principles of **purposeful, human leadership** — such as putting people and customers first, treating profit as an outcome rather than the goal — that we used then, can be applied now".

What does that really mean?

We all know that profit is the ultimate reason for the existence of a business, but learning to remember the importance of our people, particularly during tough times, is critical.

What's most important, is letting your people see that this is what you truly believe, through your actions.

How I can help. From the real world of business… the inside view.

The achievements, the sweat, the tears, and the heartache….

I've been giving Human Resources support to CEOs and leaders at all levels and leading teams for 30 years, in a wide range of industries, from Pharma, Engineering and Professional Services; in private and public sector. I've worked in many different countries, in the UK, Ireland, US, Europe and Asia.

I'm also a freelance Business Writer and Consultant, supporting the Masters programmes at the Open University, University of Law and University of Essex.

Across those contexts, many of the **same rules** apply. We talk a lot about cultures, but many actions and behaviours create the same result, and often the same problems in the workplace persist.

Being an HR leader gives a great view of the inner workings of any organisation.

How its people work, how its leaders lead, what succeeds and what fails.

The achievements, the sweat, the tears, and the heartache.

Yes, there are times when secrets are kept behind the scenes- "make sure HR doesn't find out". Secrets usually make their way to the surface, with often difficult results.

I've watched the **great** leaders and the **weaker** leaders at work. I've observed them in action, I've worked alongside them and helped them where I could, to make their lives different. Together we have improved performance.

From academic research… there's a lot out there.

As a business writer and lecturer, on the **MBA and Masters** programmes for three great online Universities, this work gives me a great window to the latest research and academic material.

I learn from my students; many are strong business leaders. They talk about their views, their struggles, and insights on what's happening in their leadership worlds every day.

II. Leading after Covid

> "History has taught us that the greatest challenges — similar to today's Coronavirus — often have a silver lining: the emergence of leaders and heroes". Reiss, 2020

What are our **hard leadership challenges** in a world where we learn how to live with **Covid?**

How do we lead differently in a world that has continued to change and evolve in so many ways?

How do the great leaders succeed, how might the weaker ones fail? What makes the difference.

How can we all learn from this? To shape and change our own approaches to be better leaders. How do we do it **better** the next time? Maybe not in a pandemic, but there are many crises to choose from.

When things don't work well, we often blame faulty approaches, systems, processes, technology- the list goes on. But mainly, if we're honest, it comes back to **how we lead and manage.**

We **can all** be **different and better**. And maybe in the distant future, after adapting to life before and after Covid, we can learn, grow and develop from what we've learned through dealing with the challenge of Covid.

But we have to be **honest** with ourselves. In those less successful situations, we did **choose** a certain path. We chose it for a reason, because of what makes us comfortable and uncomfortable.

So, if we want life to be different, we need to act and behave in a different way.

We need to make difficult, different choices.

Often that will not be easy or comfortable. In this book, let's look at some of those times when it's hard to be a leader.

I can think of many, many examples of leaders, of all ages, shapes and sizes and all levels of skill and ability. I remember the many times that they managed their people through some very difficult times. Some more successfully than others.

Covid is one of today's biggest challenges, but there are many others, and there will be harder ones for the future.

This book will help us emerge from Covid as more purposeful, human leaders.

We will look at the 10 toughest challenges for leaders in this environment.

1. Managing **anxiety**
2. Building **Trust**
3. Developing **Well-being**
4. Adapting your **vision** in the new world
5. Treating people as **individuals**
6. Sorting the **conflict**, properly
7. **Re-framing** what Covid has done.
8. New opportunities in a changing world
9. Taking a look at you- how **you** are doing?
10. **Developing** yourself in a changing world

In each of these areas I will use my HR inside lens to look at:

- How some leaders struggle.
- How some leaders succeed.

We'll look at and learn from a real-life leader, **Anna**, the Sales Manager at an IT solutions company.

- What are her leadership challenges and solutions?

For **You**- What does this mean to **you** as a leader?

- What are the practical solutions and next steps?

Who is Anna, the Sales Manager?

Anna had worked for the IT company for 5 years as a Sales Executive. She was hugely successful and developed sales to levels higher than the company ever thought possible, extending into new territories and taking new products and services into the market.

The CEO thought she was great and felt she had the talent he was looking for. Customers loved her. She was an all-round star performer.

At that time, she **only** had to worry about her own performance and didn't have to manage any people, she had very little experience of managing people.

A year ago, Anna was promoted to Sales Manager, leading a team of 6 people. The CEO believed this was a great opportunity for her to excel and show her potential.

At the start, Anna was delighted with this promotion. This was what she had been dreaming about for years. She had always felt that the bosses had the easiest jobs and didn't actually seem to do that much really.

Doesn't everyone want to be a leader!

And it would mean more money and a great career ahead, all good news, or was it?

She was given a team of, very different people with varying levels of performance and histories. People that had been her colleagues now reported to her as their manager.

The previous boss had left unexpectedly, and the plan was to put Anna in temporarily. This seemed to drift into a longer-term arrangement. She had no induction or training for the role and was straight in at the deep end.

Anna was struggling.

Although she had very little people management experience, she thought it would just come naturally. But this leading the team thing was just not working.

Some of the team weren't pleased about that.

> *Who did she think she was? She didn't really understand IT properly. Yes, it was part of her degree, but she just didn't really 'get' software. She made promises to customers but had no idea how it would be delivered.*

Covid strikes!

The Covid pandemic had made things even worse. High levels of absence, people working part of the time in the office and some working completely remotely at home and soaring anxiety levels. Being in sales, they had used Zoom for video calls before, but never to this extent. Some people loved being at home and some were hating it.

Everything was going downhill.

The poor performers had gone further downhill, and this was now harder to manage given the complexities of the whole environment. Everyone blamed everything else around them for their issues.

The CEO wasn't happy, his view was that the team was just not pulling together. He believed that remote working meant that people just were not working effectively as a team.

The subtle politics and arguments continued, this time remotely.

Anna was miserable.

But most of all ……. Anna hated her job. She was miserable. This was having a big impact on her life. She couldn't sleep at night, all the issues just kept going around in her head. She put on a lot of weight and felt so unhealthy.

Working at home with less commute should have given her more time to herself and more ability to manage her food and get some exercise.

But she just found herself working longer and longer hours without a break. And no exercise with lots of treats with her flow of coffee. Because she didn't have to drive as much, there was no reason not to have lots of wine, every day, why not? It was her only bit of fun and dulled the pain of the agony of thoughts of work!

This made her sleep worse and then hungrier on the days when she was tired. The cycle just kept on repeating, with no sign of change.

Why did she take the promotion? What should she do next?

In these next sections, we'll explore all of this.

Part 1

<u>Re-building the people.</u>

✔ Challenge No.1 Managing anxiety

"To hear the phrase "our only hope" always makes one anxious, because it means that if the only hope doesn't work, there is nothing left."

Helquist, 2004

Our only hope.

This is how we talked about our hope for a Covid vaccine, before we knew it was possible.

It was our only hope. Is it any wonder that we could see that anxiety had started running at higher levels, across all of humanity?

All of this creates a new mindset. Even the calmest amongst us have levels of anxiety unseen before. Looming economic challenges pushing us into further anxiety.

We didn't see Covid coming.

We weren't prepared. Many aren't keen to return to the office and the common view is that we won't return to the same office arrangements as before. Our high streets have continued to decline. Will they ever re-build in the same way?

How do we lead and manage our way through this?

What are the practical leadership skills and tasks in this evolving environment?

What do we need to do differently?

Let's focus on a few areas that will have the greatest impact.

With engagement, it's the <u>small</u> things that really count.

Engagement is critical.

We all know this. We've heard it before so many times. We're tired of hearing this one.

But in our new world **what** needs to be different about how we engage with our people- what do we need to do MORE of?

The leaders who struggle.

I've watched many leaders struggle with this. They go through the motions. They feel that they do their best. They send out the official comms and cascade as expected.

But they still fail on this count. They don't share the **real** information and don't really, genuinely talk on a 1-1 basis about what's going on, and how it will affect them. They don't give this the time that it needs.

Their people feel detached, at sea, unloved and confused on what's needed from them.

The number of times that I've heard the complaints-

> "I never get to hear about what is really important".

> "my boss just holds the call and goes straight to the figures",

> "my child has been really sick, and my boss never even asked how things were".

> "I'm just back from being ill and no-one understands what I've been through".

The leaders who succeed.

I've watched the **champions** of this arena at work. We often know what is deemed to be the best practice of this- there are oceans of books written about it.

But these people **actually do it**- and they keep it up, they follow through.

- They set out their stall, the explain what they're aiming for.

25

- They discuss in detail, they drive collaboration.
- They show that they take on board the feedback, they empower.
- They do it in a way that is constant, high quality and reassuring.

All the things we've heard before- but they <u>really</u> do it.

What needs to be different?

The great leaders are easy to spot, they keep in touch, ask questions that show their people that they genuinely care- not just about work, but about their lives in a broader way.

Their people say things like:

> "my manager remembered my kids' names, and they knew the tough stuff that I was working through."

> "they understood I was juggling home schooling and trying to work at the same time- but they said they appreciated my commitment by doing my best".

> "they told me early in the process so at least I had an idea about what lay ahead".

These leaders have worked out that it's not just about getting the figures and the sales into the right place- but the soft stuff matters too- and actually MORE so.

Leaders understandably find it hard to toggle between the hard and the soft stuff – their default is to be stronger in one area- and the other weaker.

But to succeed- they need to be able to work in both ways. With Covid- this has really been exposed.

Successful leaders must make time for this stuff, they must prepare well, think through the approach and talk in a meaningful and tailored way to each of their people.

In a busy world, this seems like a luxury- but in the long run it saves time because people know what they're doing, they are more likely to stay and quality of work is better- so, a time saving in the long run.

Your Task- **Tackling Challenge No.1 Engagement- Getting to know your team.**

- ✓ Look at your team- review how well you actually know them.
- ✓ Make it clear that you are committing to a new way of working with your people.
- ✓ Set up 1-1s and future diary slots for good conversations with them.
- ✓ Put a check reminder in your diary- make sure you are sharing with your people.

✔ Challenge No. 2 Building Trust

> "Hiding how you really feel and trying to make everyone happy doesn't make you nice, it just makes you a liar." **O'Connell, 2007**

The importance of building Trust is obvious and well-rehearsed.

We all know this- but this is much harder to achieve and maintain.

The leaders who struggle.

They don't get the whole concept of trust at all.

They've read about it; think they know what it means- but fail time and time again when it comes to showing their people that they trust them.

Typically, they hide information, they are accused of not being open until the very last minute.

They get tangled up in the complications around sharing information. Often there's good reason for this. It isn't always possible to share everything.

Their people feel mistrusted.

> "I never hear about what's happening until the last minute, there's just no respect".

> "We're completely ignored in all of this change".

> "Some parts of our business were closing but we were the last to know, we're just not trusted".

Often the explanation is made that the manager didn't know change was on its way. Or they didn't want to unsettle them. But it's always better to raise the flag in advance.

Ironically, leaders who think it's a good idea and "**nicer**" to pretend everything is ok, that performance is fine and there are no issues- gets the reputation that they can't be trusted. They are just not being truthful and open. This eventually comes to a head abruptly and the person doesn't get a chance to improve in a meaningful way with some time.

The person they manage is disciplined or dismissed over a short time frame. Their boss never made them aware of the issues. They lacked the courage and skill to manage their performance in a calm and useful way. Partly due to that, they lost their jobs.

In ALL organisations, **everyone** watches **everyone** else and how they're treated. And they make judgements on that basis.

When people are treated badly, everyone sees this, and they think "it will be my turn next". That's when trust starts to take a nosedive.

During the pandemic, trust has moved into a whole new arena. The changing levels of remote working meant that leaders have had to learn to trust a new way.

However, the weaker leaders struggled hugely with this approach and often implemented new levels of remote micro-management.

The leaders who succeed.

They build trust at every opportunity. Not in a false or stage-managed way In an honest way.

They ask themselves- how would I want to be treated?

They talk about tough and difficult things. If there are performance issues, they are open and honest. They handle it well.

They've built the relationship in advance to allow those conversations to take place. They talk frequently and exchange feedback on a frequent and regular basis.

They develop a coaching approach with their people. They raise the bar and expect more as part of the "growth" mind set. They help them to grow- goals are used to help move performance up and stretch them to the next level constantly. It's never about labelling or fixed ability, it's about taking them to the next level of performance Dweck, C.S. (2006).

The aim is to get to a place where feedback feels like a familiar and comfortable interaction.

They prioritise this above other things. Yes- everyone is so very busy and under pressure.

But we all choose and prioritise the things that we see as truly important- and their people see that and know it. And again, they follow through on the things that they have discussed and agreed- they don't drop them. If those leaders say they will do something, then they will do it.

They make commitments and they stick with them.

The challenges from the pandemic make these issues even more important- higher levels of remote working, increased levels of redundancies and layoffs, higher absence level, the list goes on- it's even more important than ever to succeed in building trust. It's harder now that it ever was.

Even if you don't know the whole picture- just a small part of it. Even if there's nothing to share, build trust by sharing that in an honest and open way.

That may sound a little idealistic- but there's always a way to do this- and the best leaders make it their business to focus on this. Not all of these champion leaders are perfect- they make mistakes, they mess up at times, but their people can see that they are clearly doing their best and making every effort to work closely with them.

Your Tasks **Tackling Challenge No.2 Building trust.**

- ✓ Ask yourself what you can share and plan how you will do that.
- ✓ Find out how the changing environment has impacted each individual in your team.
- ✓ Identify and clarify the issues- and the best solutions.
- ✓ Investigate sources of help for your people if they need it.
- ✓ Follow through on all commitments made.

✔ Challenge No.3 Developing Well-being

"Be the reason someone smiles. Be the reason someone feels loved and believes in the goodness in people." **Bennett, 2016**

The leaders who struggle.

They talk about Well-being as the latest fad. That mental health doesn't matter, that it's all in the head. They roll their eyes when they hear news of growing mental health issues in society.

Their people and teams see this. They observe and notice. The message they get is- don't go there.

So, they don't go there. Their people suffer in silence and when it gets really hard, they phone into work complaining of an "acceptable" health issue such as back pain. So, it never gets addressed, it's the silent issue. Time and time again.

Or maybe they pay lip service- or pretend they care about this- but whenever their people ask for help and support, maybe to book a course to help with resilience- they're refused. The leader may not laugh openly- but it's in the air. It's ignored and not taken seriously.

Crises and constant change cause inevitable stress in all our minds. And this is evident in our populations.

The leaders who succeed.

I've watched the leaders who take this seriously.

They are open about their own issues. They talk about it in a sincere and meaningful way.

35

They drive and encourage approaches to develop and increase resilience, whatever works for each person. They explain that there will always be hard times and it's about building resilience in advance of those time. Helping to build it could be just talking with their boss or colleagues, it could be the provision of outside support, made available on a direct basis to the person. There are many ways to do this- it doesn't have to cost a lot.

Having a few stronger members of staff prompted to talk openly about how they have built resilience can help to create a culture where people are willing to talk.

There are lots of books and great advice on Well-being practices- but again, it's about follow-through, and taking it seriously.

That can only be done by a leader who really means it and shows that it's genuinely important to them.

It doesn't mean being a mental health expert or counsellor- just a supporter and helper to the right places and showing that you've got their back and that you will work WITH them through the tough times.

Your Task **Tackling No. 3 Wellbeing matters**

- ✓ Set your own goals to ensure that your people are genuinely clear on how they are doing.
- ✓ Be open about how you are coping- but maintain confidence at the same time.
- ✓ Explore some tailored Wellbeing remedies and solutions- there's a lot out there.
- ✓ Identify a team member that's doing really well, use them to encourage the team to get involved with improving their wellbeing.
- ✓ Look out for creative teams to build resilience as a team such as socially distanced walks or trips when the rules allow.
- ✓ Jump into some fun leadership development activity and treks in the mountains of Ireland and the Giants Causeway
  http://www.wildirishwalks.co.uk

Anna's plan for managing higher levels of anxiety and stress.

So, what does this mean for Anna?

The sales team has never been as bad as it is now. People are worrying about worrying. Stressing about everything.

Her hunch is that some of the worst people are hidden at home. Turning up at most Zoom calls, not saying much, not turning up at others.

Anna herself has her head buried. Stressed about many other things as well as work. Home schooling definitely doesn't help. She can see sales in some areas doing well but in many they're falling fast. In this environment, who wants to spend time reviewing and updating their IT products.

So, Anna goes further into her shell of anxiety, with her fingers crossed. She doesn't reach out to connect with the hidden people working from home. She's starting to really hate Zoom.

Anna realises that something needs to change. The CEO will change her if she doesn't change. Something is going to crash here if she doesn't grab it and make it different.

Why did she ever take this role on, why did she not stay in her old sales role, with no people to manage. Life was so much simpler. She was starting to dislike her team, she knew this wasn't a good place to be.

How does Anna turn this around?

She knows that she needs to create a calm and confident atmosphere for her team to work in, that they needed to get to know her and each other, to develop real trust.

Anna knows that she needs to really understand how to work with them and lead more effectively.

She **really** wants to show her commitment to engagement with the team, to build trust and improve the wellbeing of her team. She doesn't really know how.

What Anna does next.

Anna sits up and brushes herself down.

Feeling bruised and deflated, she knows she has to act. She doesn't want to fail. She knows she's going to have to change her leadership approach if she is going to succeed.

For the first time, she makes some time for detailed planning on the areas that need work.

Anna spends some time with a trusted colleague, as a mentor, to talk through what she needs to do. They work through the bigger issues and make some outline plans. But she knows there's something missing. It doesn't feel different enough, it's avoiding some of the real issues. The truth is, she's afraid to tackle them.

Anna takes some time with her boss to discuss her plans for her team. She feels worried about saying too much and this makes her boss thinks less of her. This is a tough place for Anna.

She feels as though she's losing her mind.

Anna talks to her dad.

He's 86. He doesn't know anything about IT or about corporate life at any level. But he has experience of life and he knows how people think. He's one of those people who doesn't talk a lot, but what he does say is good, it means something.

They have a good relationship. It's not all hugs and fairy tale perfection- but good old fashion family love.

Anna confides in him and tells him all about the problems she's having.

She breaks down, she can handle crying in front of her dad. She hadn't planned to do that. She had her pride and had wanted to pretend that everything was great.

Wisdom that only the years can bring.

Her dad thinks carefully about her story before he speaks, he takes his time.

> *"Some things never change in life.*
>
> *Many things take time and effort, and some real soul searching.*
>
> *This will have to work 2 ways- you need to put in the effort and so do your team.*

*You will need to be
honest with them,
but they must also
keep their
confidence in you.*

*You must convince
them that you can
be a good leader
through thick and
thin".*

He knows Anna better than she knows herself. He knows that she's trying to hide what she doesn't know and go into her shell when she starts to panic about sorting it out.

To get past some of this she must get to know her people properly. Who they are as people, their strengths and weaknesses, their ambitions? What are their worries?

Her dad says,

*"The very most
important thing is
that they need to
know that you
care about them.*

*That you have their
back, that you'll
be there for them
whatever they
need through*

*really difficult
times.*

Her dad takes a long look at Anna and stares at her and says,

*Above everything else, you must just **always** do the right thing.*

There are no rules for that- but you will know this yourself when you ask yourself the question. You need to lead your people to think the same way.

If you do that, and your team do that, you'll never go wrong.

Anna trusts this advice from her dad. She knows he loves her and will only want the best for her.

So, Anna takes some more time to think. She concludes her detailed plan, and then makes her move.

Tackling Challenge No. 1 Engagement- Getting to know her team and Challenge No. 2 Building trust.

Anna sets up 1-1 calls with each of the team. This would be different and easier if everyone were physically in one location, in the office, but they're not.

She needs to get closer to them, to find out how they're getting on and how they would like to work differently with her. Almost a mini- survey to find out what the levels of engagement are in the changing environment.

She carefully prepares for each of those calls and has a planned and detailed structure with a set of goals for each of the calls.

Anna has come to learn that the secret to success for good calls is thorough preparation and planning and real clarity of the purpose of the call.

Anna has a different plan for each of her team. At a limited level she can see that they're all individuals and will need different things.

The 1-1 calls

Anna opens each call with an honest reflection of how she sees things going and talks about making it better.

Following through on her dad's advice and based on her detailed plan she has a long, open and engaging conversation with each of the team and explains the plan for the next calls. She commits to giving more helpful feedback on a regular basis. This is a new for her approach.

Her calls were usually highly task oriented with little recognition of their needs as people. This was going to take a while for the team to get used to.

Some were a little surprised with a conversation not completely focused on the sales task. Questions like "how are you really managing" "is there anything I can do to help support you through this", "how do you find me to work with? What are you finding difficult at the moment?"

When some of them brought up issues of juggling child care Issues, she asked how they could flex or work differently as a team to make this easier.

45

The team were not used to this level of interest in care in how to make their lives better.

She had touched on some of this before, but there was something different going on- they knew she meant it. That she would follow through on the help that they needed to do their jobs.

For Anna, a fresh start, a new relationship

This was the start of a new relationship between Anna and each of the team; this wouldn't change overnight, and the trust would need to come from showing that things would be different.

But the team were pleased and trusted that things could be different.

Tackling No. 3 Wellbeing matters for the team.

With her team, Anna took time to create a plan that was tailored to their needs.

It wasn't an expensive, medical plan. It was more about focusing on the issues that had a negative impact to their wellbeing. For example, taking time to review goals to re-size workload and focus on the ultimate and real priorities and to be clear about what could be parked.

Anna sourced a resilience building programme for the team- with individual coaching sessions and a range of classes to build practical skills.

Part 2   Re-building the team.

✔ Challenge No.4   Adapting your vision in the new world

> "The secret of change is to focus all of your energy, not on fighting the old, but on building the new." Socrates

Pulling **the team** together to succeed in the new world is crucial.

> Teams **can** thrive in difficult times, but often the pressures are too great, and they can crumble. The added challenges of remote working, extended furlough periods and threat of redundancies can just be too much to handle.

> Leaders need to ask themselves how will they keep their team together?
> What are the important things to do that will make a difference?

We know that building the vision creates the basic building blocks for strong team performance. Surely this must be impossible in the middle of a pandemic?

The leaders who struggle.

They have trouble in getting the team to work as one. This can be difficult. The many different personalities in the team and changing ways of working and thinking make this a tough area.

The pandemic has created extra challenges with the many issues that we all know so well. Many leaders have had their own home issues to deal with on top of trying to manage a team in this environment.

People have reported many of the benefits of home working, but at the same time feel more distant from their organisations and colleagues.

In all of this, the vision of the team and the organisation is forgotten, and it becomes just enough to stay afloat.

The leaders who succeed.

Crises will always happen. But the strong leader will steady the ship and get back on track at the earliest opportunity. They keep the human aspect front and centre but very closely behind that, they keep their **vision**. Maintaining this central vision is a key element that will help that team to remain as one and moving in the same direction.

They keep the vision alive in subtle ways, they bring it back when the opportunity arises in team meetings. In the midst of any crises, they revisit their plans through a review of goals and targets.

They do this in ways that feel normal and natural. It's a subtle part of team planning and discussion.

> In "Start with Why: How Great Leaders Inspire Everyone to Take Action" Simon Sinek drives us to understand that any vision should be more than a two-dimensional picture of where we are heading for.
>
> "People don't buy what you do. They buy **why** you do it. "Why" - This is the core

belief of the business. It's why the business exists".

Those great leaders pull their teams through difficult times. They keep bringing the team back to the Why? and to the vision.

We've all talked about this stuff before- but this became so much more critical when people are scattered remotely and highly anxious. The really effective leaders are highly aware of the extra challenges this brings and builds this into their planning and activities.

New and additional 1-1 calls scheduled with their people, different and creative ways of engaging are all important.

Are these people Super-human?

These leaders aren't super-human- they just prioritise well, focus and learn to work differently as leaders.

Back to the very old adage- the soft skills are everything, and they will be much more important as we learn how to live with Covid and eventually move into a better world.

Your Task to pull the team together: Check your vision.

- ✓ Keep your vision up front and central- re-visit what you have and refresh.
- ✓ Do a straw poll with your people- what do they know and remember about your vision?
- ✓ Do they remember the "whys" of your vision?
- ✓ Get ready to communicate where you're heading for.

✔ Challenge No.5 Treating people as individuals and supporting them at tough times

We're all so different and we like to be treated as people, as human beings, not a number. So, this is key for leaders in their skill set.

The leaders who struggle.

We're not all the same. The weaker leaders think they can lead everyone in exactly the same way. They don't consider the different personalities. If they do, they don't work differently with them. They don't think about the types of people they are leading. What makes them tick? They ignore whether they are introverts or extroverts?

Those leaders confuse this with fairness and equality. They think that they need to treat everyone exactly the same or be accused of unfair treatment.

We only have to look at the pandemic to see the huge variations in human behaviour. The theories and views about Covid vary widely from being super safe and maybe paranoid of the impact of Covid, right across to completely ignoring it or being a Covid "denier". Families and friends have experienced conflict about how we should behave during Covid.

This just gives us a flavour of the wide variation of the types of people on teams and how we lead and manage them.

Leaders have struggled with the reactions to Covid and been worried about the right way to deal with all the issues that fall out from it.

The leaders who succeed.

They flex their approach to the individuals in their team. Yes- people need to have the same opportunities and rights- but we should be aware that we're dealing with people with often widely differing personalities, cultures and attitudes.

These leaders get to know their people, it helps them to work this out.

They can see the differences in how their people were reacting to Covid and managed the issues accordingly. They could see that some were keen to come into the office, but many were keen to stay at home.

In terms of personality differences, they make themselves aware of the introverts, the extroverts, and the neurotics. They may not use these labels in their head - but they will have real clarity on who the people in their teams are.

It shouldn't really be needed - but some companies use elaborate and often expensive testing processes and 360-degree feedback to really build up their knowledge of their people and how they are doing.

There are many other equally effective ways of doing this. The great leaders do it naturally, just by keeping close to their people and their teams.

Many strong leaders are highly effective in the absence of any test or feedback systems- just through good old fashion strong leadership and management.

Equipped with great knowledge and awareness of their people, the great leaders can shape their approach to their activities- how they communicate, how they give feedback, how they manage performance etc, all these activities need to be tailored to the people in our teams.

Sounds like hard work and time-consuming- yes but again, it wastes more time when it's not done well.

Your Task- Who are you leading?

- ✓ Do a stock take of the individuals in your team. How do you lead and manage them?
- ✓ On a piece of paper, in a very informal way, set out:
  - ○ Who they are as individuals, what sort of people are they?
    - ▪ (don't do this on your computer, the process and formality become an obstacle to your clear thinking in this task)
- ✓ Continue to set out their strengths and weaknesses. Set out their ambitions.
- ✓ Ask yourself truly- Do you tailor how you lead them as individuals.

✔ Challenge No.6. Sorting the conflict, properly

"Courage is the most important of all the virtues because without courage, you can't practice any other virtue consistently." **Angelou, 2014**

There will always be conflict. Even the strongest teams disagree and argue.

Conflict can be very subtle and isn't noticed by many leaders, though strongly felt by people in their team. Some conflict can be healthy if it's well channelled and managed.

There are two very common types of people at the root of conflict and are particularly dangerous, the **underminers** and the **bullies**.

Teams can agree things when they are together and then leave the room and not carry through what they said they would do. They **undermine** the message in many ways. They grumble about it and debate it to peers, colleagues, and customers. One of the favourite techniques used by these people is the rolling of the eyes or the glances sideways at other colleagues when their boss is talking.

Either way, they don't hold the line and display that they clearly don't agree. Or they may be very subtle in their undermining and do it behind the scenes without being seen.

Conflict can appear in the form of **bullying** and poor treatment of individuals, both physically and mentally.

How these types of conflict are handled really separates the strong from the weaker leaders.

The leaders who struggle.

They ignore conflict, they cross their fingers and hope it will go away in time by itself. They know that stronger individuals dominate others within the team. But they let it go.

Even in meetings they can see what is going on. But they put their heads in the sand and pretend it's not happening. Meanwhile people suffer, they take their problems home at night to their families and spend time thinking about how to get a new job. They shouldn't have to.

Any leader that has managed teams will have been through these many types of conflict. There is a fine balance on the right time to intervene. But in truth, many of us know, these things happen but we maybe didn't act.

We may have made attempts. At times that may have worked.

Or we don't tackle it. People say, "you know what they're like". They are excused for their bad behaviour. Weak leaders put up with bad behaviour and its wrong.

They wonder why some things don't work when they have people who have agreed a position on something with the team, and then go away and do their own thing. Other team members see this in action and it completely undermines the leader and the changes they are trying to make.

The leaders who succeed.

They really grab the issues. They notice, they watch, and they let it be seen that they truly tackle the problem and the bad behaviours.

They do this in subtle ways when it first appears, but the team can see that there is zero tolerance of the wrong behaviours in that team. They "nip it in the bud".

If this subtle approach doesn't work more direct action is taken. During meetings good leaders will intervene if they detect repeated poor behaviour. Behind the scenes, if needed, that leader will take the time to formally sort the issue, which could include disciplinary action. They will fully follow through. They will spend time on these issues to sort them out. These are never quick processes.

Even for the more subtle undermining they will tackle it. They will "call" the behaviour and approach the person directly.

They look the perpetrator in the eye and say, "no more".

The team are left in no doubt what is acceptable. That leader genuinely models the behaviour that is expected. This is not always easy. At times we drop our guard, and we think the team is just having fun but it's at someone else's expense. A leader is never really off duty.

This is important, it's critical, it's everything.

This is by far one of the most important areas that leaders MUST succeed in, it is critical.

There can be repercussions right across team performance and behaviours. It has potential to completely undermine good team relationships and dynamics up to that point. The impact is not just on the person being treated badly, but to everyone else around them. So, it's crucial that it's sorted, properly.

Your Task to sort out the conflict, properly.

✓ Take stock of any issues burning away in the back ground in your team- write them down.
✓ Talk to your people- ask them if they feel there are unresolved issues. Work hard to get an honest answer- they are usually there.
✓ Create a plan to sort those issues.
✓ Take action, properly- don't let them simmer.

Anna's plan for pulling the team together.

So, what does this mean for Anna?

Anna knows that the lives of her customers and the market has been drastically changing around her. The pandemic has changed so much about the environment that she sells into, that she almost doesn't know how where to start.

But her people do know, they're still working closely with their customers and know what they need.

Anna and the team review their vision and plans for the business.

Anna sets up some sessions with the team to review their business and re-visit the mission for their business. Her sessions go well. They don't end up with major changes, but everyone feels that at least they have contributed and they're comfortable that they are still in the right place.

They agree a new version of the vision and the overall business plan. She and the team articulate more on the "why" of their business and this helps them with their review.

They spend a lot of time talking about the impact of Covid for their customers and solutions that will help them with their business. They agree plans to re-package and re-brand what they do differently as a result of Covid.

Anna shapes how her team works around who they are as individuals. She spends time planning and discussing with them and the roles that they all play in the team.

They all come out of this feeling that they have something different and unique to offer to the team. They had always felt that Anna wanted people just like her- so to be recognised and appreciated as different and having a unique role in the team felt good for those individuals.

Anna tackles the conflict.

The team were never overly loud or obvious in their disagreements, with her or each other.

It was worse, it was subtle, passive, and toxic. She knew she was being undermined behind the scenes, but she couldn't really put her finger on who or when.

She had lost some good team members in the last year and couldn't really understand why…. Or didn't she?

Pushing herself to be honest on this front, she knew that she herself was too different, as a person, to some of those individuals that had left, and she wasn't able to handle it.

They felt they didn't fit; they weren't like her enough. So, she was putting together a team of clones and she knew this was wrong and dangerous. She knew that she had to move to prevent this going further.

So, she put together a very informal strategy to really make this different. She then put it to the team. It was about encouraging a diverse team, with diverse thinking- and that she genuinely wanted this.

At first the team felt she didn't really mean this. But with some time, attention, and commitment to this, they could see that Anna meant business this time- that she would keep with this new approach. That most of all- she was open to challenge.

As part of this journey of change, Anna called the team members that had left over the last year. Initially they were reluctant to talk openly, but when she convinced them that she was committed and genuine in her wish for change, they opened up.

They shared with her that she as a boss was difficult to work with at times. That she wasn't approachable, and she didn't like challenge. So, they just stopped approaching her and said yes to everything she proposed.

The other big problem was one of the team who had been there for many years. They had a well-known track record of very subtle undermining of her plans behind the scenes.

Then to make matters worse, they were bullying people in the team. Their style was to be subtle, but just to say enough in meeting that people knew what they meant, but it was difficult to really accuse them of undermining the message and being bullies.

Anna asked them why they didn't bring this up before. They said that they just didn't feel able to. The bully was good at their job and seemed to be a strong part of the team, and they'd been there so long. Everyone had thought this person would have been the Sales Manager by now and was surprised when they didn't. Anna thanked them for talking to her. She was determined to create a different team culture.

Anna thought about the bully. In her heart she knew there were problems there, but they were subtle, so it was just easier to ignore. She knew there were times that she herself was bullied by the person. In agreeing goals, she let them set their own targets that she knew were too soft. When things didn't go well, she didn't manage their performance well either.

The bully actually bullied the whole team, including Anna. They constantly undermined her plans with people in the team and even with customers. They would roll their eyes and laugh with customers about the changes planned to some product changes.

Other people saw all of this and then saw Anna as a weak leader. This impacted the whole team dynamic.

Anna suddenly saw a lot of things more clearly.

This explained a lot. It made her go cold, that so much of what went on the team could be rooted back to this one relationship and this one bully. She knew she had to sort it out. She hated herself for letting this bully have their own way and control the team in subtle ways.

Anna took time to think through a careful plan of approach. She spent time with her boss to consider the plan and get buy in. She decided that the next time the bully acted up in a meeting that she would tackle it.

And this time she did. She worked through a full process with the person and eventually after repeated issues, went through a disciplinary process.

This wasn't really getting her anywhere fast and the bully just seemed to be treading water.

So, Anna, arranged a meeting with the bully. Following the pandemic rules on distancing etc and she had a strong 1-1 conversation with them.

Anna dug deep. She brought through all of the courage she could muster and told the bully what she thought of them.

She asked them if they felt they were in the right role and did they want to have a future. Maybe they needed to develop in a different role and move to something else.

She knew she was on thin ice from a technical perspective. Could she be seen as the harasser? - but she didn't care she had enough, and she needed to protect the good people in her team.

She had two more similar meetings and after some debate and icy exchanges the message seemed to be getting through. She persevered with the approach and really felt she was getting somewhere. She increased their targets to the level they should have been at, even with the current economic challenges, she still felt they should be increased.

One day, out of the blue the bully resigned. Anna was delighted and the team quietly celebrated the great news. A great result.

Life doesn't always work out this way, but good when it does. It helped Anna work on her courage for other difficult confrontations that came her way. The team increased their trust in her that she would stand by them and that she had strength as a leader.

Part 3 **Re-building the business.**

✔ Challenge No. 7 Re-framing what Covid has done

"In the face of
adversity, we have a
choice.
We can be bitter, or
we can be better.
Those words are my
North Star."
Sullivan,2015

As leaders we must create a better life. We must learn to live with Covid until it can't hurt us.

As we all know, everything comes back to mindset. It depends how you look at it. Yes, many of us have been hurt by Covid in one way of another. Maybe directly through personal illness, or tragically we've lost people to Covid that we loved. Lost business, lost opportunities, loss of living....

The list goes on in the ways many of us have been hurt. But we have no choice- to survive and prosper we must move on and prepare the world for the generations ahead of us.

The leaders who struggle.

They stay with the negative narrative of Covid, they don't work to progress or develop. It wears them down and they struggle to recover. They further depress themselves and their team more than they already are.

They live in misery about how everything has changed with no idea how to adapt or change their organisation. They remain stuck in this place and keep their teams there with them

If they don't flourish, then what chance do the people they lead have.

The leaders who succeed.

Those leaders show a genuine care and interest in what their people have been going through. They get to know in detail what's been happening with them and truly support them through it.

Alongside this, they work to psychologically move into a different place, a positive place.

Even if they're not sure, or they don't really believe in better days ahead, then as the great saying goes, they "fake it till you make it". The team needs the leader to rise above and be stronger than the issue.

They pull the team into the positive view. Focus on change and better times ahead.

Your Tasks

✓ Plan how to raise the overall mindset in your team to a more positive place.
✓ Monitor all comms and intervene carefully to re-position where possible.

✔ Challenge No. 8 New opportunities in a changing world

"Though nobody can go back and make a new beginning... Anyone can start over and make a new ending." **Xavier**

Living through the pandemic has certainly given us all lots of increased challenges.

The leaders who struggle.

They lobby pessimism about woeful times ahead. The targets of the organisation are forgotten and ignored.

They carry on as if life is unchanged and expect their organisation just to pick up exactly where it left off before Covid ever happened.

This is never a conversation these leaders have with their people. They don't see it as a relevant area to get into. They don't see their people in this way.

Their people feel that they have ideas that could help the organisation, they feel that they have a lot to offer. But, as usual, they are ignored.

The leaders who succeed.

They may talk about a "re-set", and new ways of living and working- the great leaders just get on with the positive mindset and move forward.

A vision re-set and check may be a practical step taken by those good leaders.

To look at and understand the new world- where does their business fit- what new opportunities are out there? How do they evolve to fit into that?

Those leaders involve their people in that consideration of change. They ask for their contribution in a very direct and practical way.

They make sure they know they are being brought into that discussion- that they can contribute to it.

This is a real task for those engaging leaders to really get their teeth into.

Times of great change that include pandemics, wars, major events and crises are often times that provoke further revolution and change in all sorts of ways. When we look back in history, this has happened time and time again.

As we know "necessity is the mother of invention" and this level of change will no doubt trigger many other innovations and inventions right across society.

Some will fall by the way side. The obvious radical decline of the high street is triggering a whole range of other channels of how people sell their goods.

This is a great time to keep the good parts of our different way of working. What has worked well and what do we keep after Covid becomes just a part of everyday life.

This is a good time to reward your people for new innovative ideas. Going above and beyond should be recognised and even if it's only small gestures of appreciation can mean a lot to your people.

Your Tasks

- ✓ Work with the team to drive innovation and take advantage of new opportunities in a changing world.
- ✓ Plan some reward activity linked to resilience and values, ensure they are tailored carefully to the individuals.

Anna's plan for creating a better life after Covid.

So, how does Anna re-frame and change the mindset?

Anna knows that she must create a more positive mindset with the team. Yes, she can work to fix as many of the background issues as she can, but Covid has had such a negative impact on the overall morale of the team and they're just feeling low.

What can she do about this?

It depends on timing- how far along will the team be with the big issues at home. How many of their family circle will have had vaccines, how many will have had health issues caused by Covid.

Not an easy one, and it needs to be sensitive to everything in the team's home lives. This was a delicate process, and it could go badly wrong if it was timed badly.

Anna picked her time carefully and she started to move her communications with the team into a positive frame. She felt that the team was in a reasonable place.

Armed with her new vision she started to really value and cherish her team to have a more optimistic mindset. With every piece of comms, she asked herself, how can I re-position this?

Anna placed a focus on keeping the good parts of the new ways of working. Did some people want to maintain a higher level of home working- how could she work with them to support this and make it possible?

The secret was to demonstrate that she would do her very best to keep those things that really worked for them.

She looked at some ways that she could introduce some small rewards for the team. Working with her boss she agreed a small budget to buy some vouchers and small gifts.

Anna spent some careful time with the team to explore the type of rewards they would appreciate. They came up with some small ideas such as pizza deliveries for their family at home, plants for the garden for those with an interest in gardening and exercise equipment for the fitness follower.

She picked a logical point in the calendar, at financial year end and then introduced the rewards tied to achievements linked to their team and company values. Things that also showed their input for new opportunities for the business, resilience and their work to keep the team working successfully together.

She wrote a thoughtful note to each of them and tied a reward to it. Something that was really tailored to each of the team.

Part 4 Re-building You.

✔ Challenge No. 9 Take a look at you- how you are doing now?

"Believe in yourself. You are braver than you think, more talented than you know, and capable of more than you imagine." **Bennett, 2016**

Surely something good has to come out of all of this.

We've all been forced to sit back and look at our lives and our surroundings. People have done this in a way that they have never done before. Many of us haven't had the time and space to do this before. Some of this space became crowded very quickly with the need to survive and keep our heads above water.

No matter what our occupation or everyday lives look like, we've paused and asked ourselves what it's all about.

Life goes by in a blink, normally we don't take stock or reflect on what we want. We're busy surviving and keeping afloat.

We have to take advantage of that thinking. In our working lives we take time to reflect on how the business is going and how the people are coping- what about ourselves- we need to reflect on how we are in the same way.

So- how are you doing?

How does everything look compared to a year or 2 years previous, or even 10 years ago?

Ask yourself that question.

What is the answer and what do you want to do about it?

If you feel that some parts of your life have improved in some ways- how do you keep those aspects? What action do you need to take?

If you don't value anything about how your life may have changed – then where do you go next? What action is needed?

There are some great, big questions in this, important ones.

The leaders who struggle.

They will just pick up where they left off. They don't take advantage of the new thoughts or changed ways of life that they have experienced.

They will work with their team as if nothing has ever happened and it will not be discussed or spoken about when normality of some type returns.

These leaders ignore the warning signs. They ignore the health issues that have appeared. These can be psychological issues with increased levels of anxiety experiences, or physical changes such as lower levels of fitness and weight gain with less activity.

The leaders who succeed.

These leaders take time to sit back and consider how they are, they look after themselves.

They consider where they are on the bigger picture of their life and career plans.

How does this all fit together? How do all of these new ways of working fit in with their families, friends, and activities that they like to do in their spare time.

If it doesn't feel right and it doesn't fit with the overall plan, they act.

If they find that physical or psychological symptoms have appeared, then they act.

Those successful leaders will build in coping mechanisms and time out to work on anxiety. They manage their diets and increase exercise levels to look after their health.

They will look at how their work has changed and think about solutions to improve the problem areas.

That action might mean talking to their boss to plan how to change their roles or look at resourcing needs.

Your Tasks

- ✓ Take some time to really reflect on how you have been coping.
- ✓ How is your health physically and mentally- has it changed?
- ✓ What actions to you need to take to make it different?

✔ Challenge No. 10 Developing yourself as a leader in a changing world.

"The only way that we can live, is if we grow.

The only way that we can grow is if we change.

The only way that we can change is if we learn.

The only way we can learn is if we are exposed.

And the only way that we can become exposed is if we throw ourselves out into the open.

Do it.

Throw yourself."

JoyBell

Stronger and better.

Your goal must be to come through this stronger and better, how do you achieve that?

Based on everything that we have talked about so far in this book, there are signposts in this book to help you reflect on the areas that may need your attention.

Does this new, changing world need **new** skills and abilities? Do you need to change and develop in line with that? Look at how the world is evolving in our environment.

It will only be the people who know how to evolve and equip themselves to adapt to their changing environments that will ultimately succeed and do well.

Some of those changes in **how** we work, the increase in **home** working, the **decline** of the high street and the ongoing economic challenges have radically increased the need for new and different skills for all of us.

We will all need to be much more digitally literate and help those around us to be the same. Those who get left behind will suffer as a result.

As leaders we must view our businesses in that light to make sure it is competitive.

The leaders who struggle.

They will expect their usual ways of working to continue to make them successful in a changing world. They will just keep doing what they've done before.

They will ignore the need for different skill sets for both themselves and their people.

The leaders who succeed.

These leaders take time to sit back and consider their skill gaps in the midst of all the changes.

They also consider how this impacts the bigger picture of their life and career plans. How does this all fit together?

They make sure that their plan for their lives has a strong focus on making sure that they have done the things that they wanted to do, and it hasn't been all about work.

Your Tasks

- ✓ Identify your skills gaps in the changing world that we're in.
- ✓ Note those gaps and create a plan to manage your own development.
- ✓ Reflect on your bigger life picture- has this changed- do you need to change your plans?

Anna's plan to improve her own life.

Anna hasn't been happy for a while.

But she sees signs of improvement. The steps she's taken to build the team and look at the new opportunities for change in the business have brought her to a better place.

She knows she still has a lot to do and there is a lot more change ahead, most of which she can't see yet.

Anna looks at her own skills and asks herself where her shortfalls are. She always knew that her understanding of the technology in her business was lacking, both inside the business and with the products and services she sold to her customers. She accepted too that the increased level of digital activity right across society meant that she just had to bring these skills into a much stronger place.

So, she decided to enrol for learning that would tackle some of those weak spots. This would increase the credibility she had with the team as she would understand more about how it all worked. It would also put her into a better place career wise as she would need a better grasp of the digital world if she wanted to move company.

Anna thinks about some of the things that she had talked about in her 1-1s with her team.

She knew that she had a certain sort of personality that didn't inspire the team at times and that she would need to do something about that. She talked about this with her own boss and her colleague and she went back to her dad again.

She was looking for some "plain talking" again and some real advice about how to change how she came across.

Anna's dad listened to the detail of the issues that she had with the team and some of the feedback that they gave her on how she led them.

In his usual way, her dad gave her a few words of wisdom.

He said that becoming fully accepted as the leader of their team would take time. It would mean working on some parts of her personality and style that just didn't work at times. She didn't have the option to go into her shell when things weren't going well, she had to keep out there and be resilient for the team when they needed her. She couldn't crumble and hide when she didn't feel good about her leadership.

Her dad shared with her that she tended to do this as a child, and some habits are hard to change. Even when she was small, she would run away and hide if things weren't going her way.

He said that changing this would make a difference, not just to her work, but to the rest of her life.

Anna took it on the chin.

She knew that strong leaders didn't have the option of running away when the going got tough. Her team had spotted this in her and they had lost her trust in her ability to lead them. Anna knew that she had a lot to learn but this was certainly one of the biggest issues.

Her dad came through again in helping her to face up to what she needed to change. How would she ever cope without him?

But at this point in her life, Anna had all she needed to carry her through to the next stages of the pandemic. To survive, and even more, to succeed.

Happier now that her team
was with her, she felt
confident to move ahead
and shape her team and
business to cope with
where Covid would take
them to next.

Conclusion.

Covid has thrown a very large, curved ball to
leaders of all types.

There is no doubt, this has been tough in so many
different ways.

This ball has broken many of us, many
businesses have gone to the wall, many people
have crashed and burned.

There has been a lot to adjust to and a lot to learn
as a leader.

We've talked about the four big areas that are
important for leaders to give their attention to:

- **Re-building the people** by managing
  anxiety and stress; by building trust across
  their teams, re-building relationships at all
  levels and finally by making sure that a
  good wellbeing plan surrounds the health
  of the team.

- **Re-building the team** by re-visiting the vision, is it fit for purpose and talking about that with the team; by treating the people in the team as individuals, making sure you understand them and their needs fully; by sorting the conflict truly and properly, not in a superficial way.

- **Re-building the business**; re-framing what Covid has done, helping to re-set the narrative with the team and the relationships with the customers that they support; taking advantage of new and different opportunities and being innovative.

- **Re-building You;** taking a good look at yourself- how have you changed, what's better or worse; developing yourself in a changing world, what do you need to learn or do differently.

What Anna has taught us.

As we have walked through these four big areas, we have looked at the world of Anna, the Sales Manager, and how she has learned and developed differently as a leader.

By working with Leaders like Anna, who work hard to adapt and lead their teams in a caring and honest way, we've learned a lot about what works in practice.

Anna's willingness to open up to expose her weaknesses has been important and the first step in real learning for her.

Talking to other people around her that she could trust, meant that she could help herself understand how she needed to change and most importantly, how she needed to develop.

The leaders who struggle and those who succeed.

I often reflect on those great leaders and weaker leaders that I have worked with over 30 years in HR.

I think about the things that I have watched unfold before my eyes- the good and the bad.

It does truly amaze me that there are so many constant principles, behaviours and values that are always there.

Time and time again, they appear in those leaders who are the greatest successes.

Back at the start of my career, many of those same challenges were there, and now today in living with Covid, many of the same leadership issues remain. They are still there. It's startling how much of it remains true.

So, with all of that it can be hard to understand why the leaders who struggle don't learn the important lessons. Probably because they find it too difficult to change and be different, no matter what the situation or environment.

As we know, it's all about the choices that we make.

They may not be conscious choices, but we certainly make them, one way or another.

We all do it, every day. We choose how to behave with our partners, our friends, our families, and that has its consequences, for better and worse.

And finally- You're alive.

At the start of this book, we talked about the early days of the pandemic when we didn't even know if we could create a vaccine, and the first levels of anxiety, which for many has continued. For some it has got worse.

As Covid starts to reduce its grip, no doubt our looming economic troubles, high street decline and learning to work away from the office at a greater level will continue to throw us all leadership challenges.

And who knows what else to deal with,

To be a "Leader who succeeds"

I trust that this book and my experiences as an HR leader have helped you to understand more about the behaviour of the Leaders who struggle and those who succeed.

Your final task to self is to write down and commit to your final "to do list".

At the top of this must be to how you look after yourself, this must come first.

That you will develop yourself to cope with this world as it continues to change after Covid.

I have no doubt that if you do these things you will be a **"Leader who succeeds."**

And then the sun came out.

But at least if you're reading this book, you're **alive**.

And that's something to be very grateful for.

We're safe, in one piece.

Good to feel those warm rays coming through.

"Write it on your heart,

that every day is the best day in the year.
He is rich who owns the day, and no one owns the day
who allows it to be invaded with fret and anxiety.

Finish every day and be done with it.
You have done what you could.
Some blunders and absurdities, no doubt crept in.
Forget them as soon as you can, tomorrow is a new day;
begin it well and serenely, with too high a spirit
to be cumbered with your old nonsense.

This new day is too dear,
with its hopes and invitations,
to waste a moment on the yesterdays."

Emerson, 1994

About the Author

Hi there,

Thank you for taking time to read my book. I hope you enjoy it.

I'm a freelance Business Writer and Consultant, supporting the Masters programmes at the Open University, University of Law and University of Essex.

I've given Human Resources support to CEOs and leaders at all levels for 30 years. I have previously led global teams at director level, in a wide range of industries, from Pharma, Engineering and Professional Services, in private and public sector. I have worked in many different countries, from the UK, Ireland and the US, Europe to Asia.

My ongoing projects and passions focus on Employee Engagement and relations, Performance Management and Global Talent Acquisition and Development. I have helped companies to be accredited as Sunday Times Best Companies and Investors in People Gold with World Class people practices recognition.

Some of my current work is with Wild Irish Walks www.wildirishwalks.co.uk where we have been developing some great leadership development activities and treks in the mountains of Ireland and the Giants Causeway.

I'm MSc qualified in Organisation Development, Coaching and Leadership and HRM, I also hold a BSc Occupational Psychology and Careers Guidance and have qualifications in Business Management and Lean Process re-engineering.

> Being an HR leader gives a **great view of the inner workings** of any organisation. How its people work, how its leaders lead, what succeeds and what fails.
>
> The achievements, the sweat, the tears, and the heartache.

> I've watched the **great** leaders and the **weaker** leaders at work. I've observed them in action, I've worked alongside them and helped them where I could, to make their lives different. Together we have improved performance.

After many years of working at the HR coalface I wanted to share some of what I have learned about the leaders that I've worked with. ☺

Big Thanks

Thank you to my wonderful husband Phil for your love and support. 🩶

Thank you to my great family and friends who always give the very best love, help and morale uplift.

To my very precious mum and dad, who aren't with us today, their values built this book.

*Thank you to Mhairi Braden, my wonderful, talented illustrator niece, who designed the front cover of this book https://www.mhairibraden.com/

Sources

Maya Angelou, M. (2014) Maya Angelou quotes: 15 of the best (online) https://www.theguardian.com/books/2014/may/28/maya-angelou-in-fifteen-quotes

Bennett, R.T. (2016) The Light in the Heart, Kindle, Bennett, London

Chapman, Bob (December 5, 2012). "Walk Your Talk". Retrieved from https://www.trulyhumanleadership.com/?p=356&p=356

Dweck, C.S. (2006) *Mindset: The New Psychology of Success* New York: Random House

Emmerson, R.W. (1994). Collected Poems and Translations, Library of America, New York

Helquist, B. (2004) Series of Unfortunate Events: The Blank Book (A Series of Unfortunate Events), HarperCollins Publishers, New York

Ibarra, I and Scoular, A, 2019, The Leader as Coach, https://hbr.org/2019/11/the-leader-as-coach (online)

Joly, H 2020, A Time to Lead with Purpose and Humanity (online) https://hbr.org/2020/03/a-time-to-lead-with-purpose-and-humanity

O'Connell, J. (2007). The Book of Luke, MTV Publishing, New York

Reiss, R (2020) CEO Quotes On Leading Through This Pandemic (online) https://www.**forbes**.com/sites/robertreiss/2020/07/22/ceo-quotes-on-leading-through-this-pandemic/?sh=1ccbdf0839f2

Sinek, S. (2013). Start with why: How great leaders inspire everyone to take action, Penguin, London.

Sullivan, C (2015 Bitter Or Better: Grappling with Life on the Op-Ed Page, Rockstarpaper press, Minneapolis.